SERMON OUTLINES FOR

Growing Christians

By Stephen M. Hooks

Standard Sermon Starters

Sam E. Stone, Editor

STANDARD
PUBLISHING
Cincinnati, Ohio

The Standard Publishing Company, Cincinnati, Ohio
A division of Standex International Corporation

© 1996 by The Standard Publishing Company
All rights reserved
Printed in the United States of America

03 02 01 00 99 98 97 96   5 4 3 2 1

Library of Congress Cataloging-in-Publication Data

ISBN 0-7847-0527-5

Table of Contents

So Help Me, Me

Hebrews 6:13-20

Introduction

Life has taught us that "promises are made to be broken." For this reason we have learned to take most of them with a grain of salt. Yet the Christian faith calls us to stake our eternal destinies upon the promises of God. For this reason it is important that we understand the nature of those promises and how they are realized in our lives.

I. God's Immutable Purpose.

God wanted to make the unchanging nature of his purpose very clear to the heirs of what was promised (Hebrews 6:17).

A. God's promises are credible.
1. God's promises are grounded in His character. He has the absolute ability and the uncompromising integrity to fulfill them. They are, therefore, completely credible.
2. So important is it to God that His children believe in His promises that He on several occasions confirmed them by a sacred oath. He has voluntarily sworn by the highest power in the universe—Himself (Genesis 22:16; Isaiah 45:23; Jeremiah 22:5). It is as if God raises His right hand to us and says, "I will keep my promises, so help Me, Me!"
3. God's promise and God's oath are "two unchangeable things" (v.18). They are fixed and immutable. They are as certain as the setting of the sun (Jeremiah 33:20,21).

B. God's promises are conditional.
1. Yet, as our author has repeatedly warned, not all of God's children "inherit what has been promised" (Hebrews 6:12). This is not due to any failing on the part of God. It is due to some failing on the part of man.
2. Attached to God's promises to man are his expectations of man. One may see this all through scripture. It was true of his promise to David (1 Kings 2:4; 1 Kings 9:4-7). It was true of his promises to Israel through Moses (Deuteronomy 4:23ff). And, in the example which the author cites here, it was true of his promise to Abraham.
3. The condition which the author says the believer today must

7

meet if he is to enjoy the fulfillment of God's promises is "patience" (v.15). As God made Abraham wait for his child of promise, so also does God make us wait to see the ultimate fulfillment of his promises. By this the genuineness of our faith is "tested."

II. Man's Immovable Prospect.

God did this so that . . . we who have fled to take hold of the hope offered us may be greatly encouraged. We have this hope as an anchor for the soul, firm and secure (Hebrews 6:18,19).

There is nothing more Christian than hope. Along with faith and love, it is one of the three principle graces of the Christian life (1 Corinthians 13:13). We are a people who are "saved by hope" (Romans 8:24) and who live "resting on the hope of eternal life" (Titus 1:2).

A. The character of Christian hope.
    1. Those cheerful expressions—"all will be well," "look on the bright side," "hope for the best"—that we often use are mostly just sentiment, wishful thinking, empty optimism. The paths of life are strewn with the victims of such misplaced and ungrounded hope.
    2. Christian hope, however, is not based upon the empty wishes of men but upon the nature and character of God. As long as our hope is founded in Him, it will never fail us, it will never let us down.

B. The consequences of Christian hope.
    1. Hope is the Christian's asylum. As the ancient Israelite could cling to the altar in hope of redemption, so can the believer cling to hope as a temporary asylum until the time of our final vindication (v. 18).
    2. Hope is the Christian's anchor. It functions like a spiritual mooring to bind us to the "Rock of our salvation" (v. 18; Psalm 95:1).

Conclusion

We have an anchor that keeps the soul
  Steadfast and sure while the billows roll,
Fastened to the Rock which cannot move,
  Grounded firm and deep in the Savior's love.

Loved by Perfection
Hebrews 12:4-13

Introduction

It is hard to be loved by perfection. As a virtuoso pounces upon the keys of a piano determined to summon forth its most resonant sounds; as a sculptor furiously chips away at a large piece of marble intent on releasing the image of beauty that hides within it; so also does the Creator lay His hand upon our lives determined to lift us to our spiritual potential. It is hard to be loved by perfection.

I. The Father's Affection for His Children

"The Lord disciplines those he loves . . . God is treating you as sons"
(Hebrews 12:6,7).

A. The Bible paints many portraits of God and how He relates to humankind.
   1. He is the Creator, we are the creatures.
   2. He is the Sovereign, we are His subjects.
   3. He is the Shepherd, we are His sheep.

B. But the greatest biblical model of the divine-human encounter is that of a Father and His children.
   1. He is the commanding Father (Deuteronomy 14:1ff).
   2. He is the protective Father (Exodus 4:22-23; Deuteronomy 1:31).
   3. He is the providing Father (Luke 11:1-13).
   4. He is the forgiving Father (Luke 15:11-32).

C. The idea of God's "Fatherhood" owes its origin to the patriarchal culture of biblical times.
   1. The Jews of Jesus' day lived in a world dominated by the influence of fathers.
   2. When the author calls God their father, to his readers this meant that He was a benevolent authority figure who acted toward his children in sovereignty and love. A father disciplines his children because he loves them.

II. The Father's Correction of His Children

"Endure hardship as discipline . . . God disciplines us for our good"
(Hebrews 12:7,10).

A. Why do the righteous suffer? The Bible does not ignore this
   question. In fact it offers a number of possible answers.
   1. We live in a fallen world (Genesis 3:14ff; Romans 8:18-25).
   2. We are "tested" by suffering (Job 2:8-12;3:3-10; Zechariah
      13:9; 1 Peter 4:12ff).
   3. We are "matured" by suffering (James 1:2-4; Romans 5:3-4).
   4. God can be glorified in our suffering (John 9:1ff).

B. These Hebrew Christians are being persecuted by a world hostile
   to their faith (v. 4; 10:32-34).
   1. The author says that God is using this persecution to chas-
      ten his children and to bring them to spiritual maturity.
   2. This is suffering as a negative means to a positive end. God
      is permitting and even employing their suffering to summon
      forth holiness, righteousness and peace.

Conclusion

Only a fool would pretend to understand suffering fully and only a
sadist would claim to enjoy it. But this at least can be said. There is in
the struggles of life a catalyst for spiritual development which no other
force can supply. Pain has the power to summon forth from us that
which we find most difficult to surrender—uncompromising faith in
God and unqualified love for God.

Illustrations

C.S. Lewis describes the roll of suffering in the life of the believer as
"soul-making." It is the shaping of the Christian with the hammer and
chisel of adversity. Lewis also said "God whispers to us in our plea-
sures; speaks in our consciences; but shouts in our pains."

The Reluctant Missionary

Jonah 1-4

Introduction

When the name "Jonah" is mentioned, most people immediately think of a man being swallowed by a great fish. Yet this remarkable event is really only a minor part of a much more important story.

The book of Jonah is really the story of a missionary—a reluctant missionary. It is the story of a man who tried to set himself up as the judge of who is worthy to receive God's pardon. In response to God's call Jonah began running:

I. Running From God (chapter one)

A. Jonah's disobedience was a sin of omission. It was willful refusal to answer God's call. True obedience often involves more than what we avoid doing. It also involves our positive response to God's call to service.

B. God held Jonah accountable for his refusal to answer His call.
  1. Jonah's attempt to defy God was futile. Where does one run in an attempt to get away from God?
  2. God's judgment of Jonah was appropriate to his sin. The one fleeing is trapped. The means of his attempted escape (the sea) becomes the instrument of his punishment.

II. Running Toward God (chapter two)

A. Jonah's repentance was motivated by God's judgment.
  1. The consequences of his sin forced him to reconsider the error of his ways.
  2. Sometimes we, like Jonah, must suffer the consequences of our sin before we are ready to repent.

B. Jonah's repentance was motivated by God's mercy.
  1. Notice that Jonah's prayer thanks God for a deliverance already begun. The creature which the Lord "provided" had saved Jonah from drowning and anticipated a greater deliverance to come.
  2. Likewise, God delivers us from the full consequences of our sin as an invitation to seek his even greater pardon.

III. Running With God (chapter three)

A. Jonah received a second chance to obey God's calling.
   1. God is a God of "second chances." He does not quickly give up on his children.
   2. God is responsive to our repentance. When we seek his mercy, he does not begrudge it.

B. When Jonah obeyed God's call and cooperated with His will, his ministry was blessed with power and success.
   1. At the preaching of a Hebrew prophet a hostile, pagan nation was led to repentance.
   2. The power of God's word to change lives is often released through a life that has fully submitted to His will.

IV. Running Ahead of God (chapter four)

A. Jonah second-guesses God.
   1. He resents God's offer of grace to Israel's enemies. Jonah is an intolerant nationalist who wishes to see his nation's enemies destroyed, not saved.
   2. The Ninevites have been brutally dominating Israel for decades. Jonah wants God to repay them, to give them what they deserve.

B. God censures Jonah's intolerance and prejudice.
   1. Through the incident of the withered vine, God shows Jonah that He, not Jonah, decides who shall receive His grace.
   2. Our responsibility is not to decide who is worthy to receive God's pardon. Our responsibility is to proclaim God's pardon.

Conclusion

The church today still has its reluctant missionaries—church members, who by their prejudices and judgmental attitudes, seek to limit the proclamation of the gospel to "all the nations." When we are tempted to put limits on God's grace and boundaries on his forgiveness, let us remember the lesson of Jonah.

What is Man?

Psalm 8

Introduction

"What is man?" The question of the psalmist as he stood gazing at the heavens is still a matter of some mystery today.

On the one hand we see man feeding the hungry, caring for the sick, and singing the praises of God. On the other hand we see him ignoring his starving brother, bombing his enemies, and cursing God with every breath. You and I are members of the same human race to which Cain, Judas, and Adolf Hitler belonged. "What is man?"

The Bible answers this question from at least three different perspectives.

I. The Man We Were—We are Creatures

A. We were created by God.

1. According to scripture our existence is not the result of blind chance or some mindless natural process. We are the direct result of God's creative activity. "You have made us," said the psalmist (Genesis 1:26-28;2:7).

2. Our existence is, therefore, purposeful. Our lives have meaning.

B. We were crowned by God.

1. The psalmist emphasizes the exalted state humans share by virtue of God's creation. We are a "little lower" than divine, crowned with "glory" and "honor."

2. Our worth as humans is not relative to our perceived value to our fellow humans. Our worth is absolute, established and proclaimed by the God who made us.

II. The Man We Have Become—We are Fallen Creatures

A. The Bible has no illusions about fallen humankind.

1. While declaring the dignity which man has by creation, it is also clear to expose the degradation to which he can stoop.

2. The same psalmist elsewhere confesses, "Against you, you only, have I sinned and done what is evil in your sight" (51:4).

3.   Other biblical writers affirm man's sin (Romans 3:9,10,23; I John 1:8).

B.   According to the scriptures humans are personally responsible for the evil which we do.
1.   It is characterized as rebellion against God (Genesis 3).
2.   It is the source of many of the great tragedies which befall us and rob us of our joy. Our lives are something far less than they could be because we are something far less than we could be.

III. The Man We Can Be—We are Redeemed Creatures

A.   The man we can be is really the man we were created to be.
1.   "If anyone is in Christ, he is a new creature" (2 Corinthians 5:17). There is a sense in which redemption is recreation. It is the recovery of our created natures.
2.   The final biblical portrait of redeemed humanity pictures the saved back in God's presence, free to partake of the tree of life (Revelation 22:1-5).

B.   This was the purpose for which Christ came.
1.   Jesus believed in man. He was able to look beyond our perversities to see our possibilities.
2.   The common people heard him gladly because to Him they were not common. He was constantly reminding people of their worth in God's eyes.

Conclusion

A famous artist once took his easel to the heart of Paris. He secured a studio overlooking a back street. His attention was captured by a man below—a common derelict, dirty and unshaved, spending most of his days in a drunken stupor. He decided to paint him, but not as a bum. He painted him clean, well-groomed, an image of self-respect. Then he showed the portrait to the man. "That's not me," he said. "It can't be." Replied the artist, "When I look at you, this is the man I see."

"If that is the man you see," said the derelict, "then that is the man I will be."

God honors us by seeing us not just as we are, but as we can be. For "while we were still sinners . . ." (Romans 5:8).

Rediscovering the Bible

2 Kings 22:8—23:2

Introduction

In 1947 some Bedouin shepherds accidentally stumbled upon the most important biblical manuscripts to be discovered in modern times—the Dead Sea Scrolls. These priceless copies of Holy Scripture had been hidden, unknown to man for nearly 2000 years. If you can imagine the excitement surrounding this discovery, then you will begin to appreciate the excitement surrounding the incident our text records.

I. A Timely Discovery

A. In 638 B.C. a new man ascended the throne of the kingdom of Judah.

1. Up to this point Judah's history had been a chronicle of a sorry succession of weak, unscrupulous rulers.

2. A single verse describes their reigns, recurring like a doleful refrain throughout the book of Kings, "and he did what was evil in the sight of the Lord."

B. But suddenly the rhythm breaks and there comes to the throne one of whom the chronicler can say, "He did what was right in the eyes of the Lord . . . and did not turn aside to the right hand or the left" (2 Kings 22:20).

1. So begins the reign of Josiah, one of Judah's noblest kings.

2. On Josiah's 26th birthday his life took a dramatic turn. He decided to rebuild the temple which had fallen into a state of disrepair. By rebuilding that sacred shrine he hoped to restore the religion that the temple symbolized.

C. However, it was not a rediscovered building that was to bring religious revival to the land, but a rediscovered book.

1. A group of workmen discovered an old scroll that had been hidden beneath the debris.

2. Imagine the excitement of Josiah as the scroll is read to him, the growing awareness that this was no ordinary book, the final realization that this was nothing less than the law of God.

3. There followed the greatest religious revival in Judah's history.

II. A Timeless Truth

A. This story can be read almost as a parable.

    1. Throughout history the Bible has often been a lost book, buried and forgotten beneath the rubble of ignorance, tyranny, and unbelief.

    2. It was so before the invention of printing, in pre-reformation Europe, and tragically it is also true today when, in spite of the fact that it remains the world's most widely distributed book, it is seldom read and is regarded by many as mythical or outdated.

B. But each and every time that the Bible has been rediscovered it has invariably resulted in changed lives and revitalized religion.

    1. The renewals, reformations, and revivals in the history of the church can be traced, almost without exception, to one factor—some fresh rediscovery of some essential message of the Bible.

    2. When the church has wandered from the Gospel into the paths of its own devising, a new and deep study of Scripture has been the means of recalling it to the truth and purpose of God.

    3. The great giants of the faith, whose influence has shaped the course of Christian history, for the most part, have derived their motivation from a renewed contact with the written word.

C. But the greatest power of Scripture is not its ability to start movements; it is its ability to change lives. What can a rediscovery of the Bible mean for us?

    1. Ask a man on his death bed who has read of the "resurrection and the life."

    2. Ask a widow at a graveside who is reminded that "the Lord is my shepherd."

    3. Ask a lonely, guilt-ridden sinner who has at last discovered the "God who so loved the world."

Conclusion

Whittier said it well in a bit of oft-repeated verse: "We search the world for truth, we cull the good, the pure, the beautiful; and weary seekers of the best, we come back, laden from our quest, to find that all the sages said, is in the Book our mothers read."

The Waiting God

2 Peter 3:9

Introduction

If patience is a virtue, it is one virtue modern man has lost. In this "up-to-the- minute" world there are very few things for which we are willing to wait. Somewhere in our headlong rush into the future we have forgotten how to wait.

In direct contrast to this is the unanimous testimony of scripture that the Almighty Creator of the universe is a God who waits. For a people who have lost the meaning of the word it is sometimes hard to understand.

I. The Mystery of God's Patience

A. God's patience was hard for the early church to understand.

1. God had made certain promises about the future and, as yet, nothing had happened. Scoffers were beginning to arise saying, "Where is this 'coming' he promised?" (v. 4).

2. Some Christians were growing impatient, and some were actually considering falling away from the church.

B. Peter writes to correct their mistaken notions about God's "slowness" to act.

1. He points out that God does not see time as we do. To the eternal Creator "a day is like a thousand years, and a thousand years are like a day" (v. 8).

2. God's patience does not imply His powerlessness. His is a power which intentionally withholds itself for the benefit of man.

3. God's patience does not imply His abandonment of His children. The parables of Jesus make it clear that God's patience is purposeful. Jesus frequently tells stories of a farmer or master who travels to a far country leaving his goods in the hands of servants and who, as often as not, delays his return, waiting to see what His servants will do in His absence.

C. When we clamor for God to do something and do it now, we need to remember that His perspective on what needs to be done and when may be quite different from our own.

II. The Meaning of God's Patience

A. God waits with a benevolent kindness that lets us share in His work.

1. At the heart of our impatience with others is the idea that "I could do it better and faster and better myself."

2. Think of how tempting that thought must be to God! There is nothing that we can do that God could not do far better and much more quickly. Yet He invites us to participate in the unfolding of His saving will. If we are impatient with God, how much more impatient He must be with us.

B. God waits because His coming will end all things.

1. This text is set against a throne of judgment. When He finally comes, He will come to judge. There will be a finality to it which will end all opportunities for repentance.

2. Instead of resenting God's patience we should rejoice in it. It continues to give us and those we love the opportunity to escape His judgment.

C. God waits because He loves us and wants us all to be saved.

1. The church has clamored for God's coming many times in its history. But God has waited, and millions more have responded to the gospel.

2. It is really not God who keeps us waiting, but we who keep Him waiting by our resistance to His saving truth.

Conclusion

With every tick of the clock of eternity that God in His patience allows He is saying, "I love you and I want you to be saved." He stands at the door and knocks waiting for us to answer. We have made Him wait long enough.

Illustration

Martin Luther could not understand how God could be so patient with men. He said that if he were God and the world had treated him as it treated God, he would have kicked the wretched thing to pieces. I'm glad that Martin Luther was not God.

George Bernard Shaw was once asked what he would have done if he were in charge when the great flood came and his reply was, "I would have let them all drown!"

Honest to God

Hebrews 4:12,13

Introduction

The Emperor's New Clothes, by Hans Christian Andersen is a humorous parody on pretense. (Tell the story).

Our text from the book of Hebrews echoes the message of this parable. It is foolish to pretend, to clothe ourselves with insincerity, to represent ourselves as other than what we are. Sooner or later, we will be exposed. We live before a God who sees us, not as we pretend to be, but as we really are.

I. Exposed by God

Nothing in all creation is hidden from God's sight. Everything is uncovered and laid bare (Hebrews 4:13).

A. Sin leads to pretention.
   1. The first thing Adam and Eve did after they ate of the forbidden fruit was to hide. They hid from each other and they hid from God. In so doing they personify fallen humankind. According to the Bible we hide because we sin.
   2. Some people spend all their days hiding. Their lives are nothing but a charade, a great hypocrisy.

B. Sin is ultimately exposed.
   1. God looks behind our masks determined to deal with the real person. God "finds us out." As the apostle Paul says in 1 Corinthians 4:5, "He will bring to light what is hidden in darkness and will expose the motives of men's hearts."
   2. The instrument of this divine exposé of men is the living and active word of God. Like sharp daggers, God's commands pierce our pretensions to disclose our true level of trust and commitment. The double-edged sword of the word not only reveals God to man, it reveals man to God.

II. Examined by God

". . . before the eyes of him to whom we must give account" (Hebrews 4:13).

A. Modern man has difficulty believing in a God "to whom we must give account." Culturally conditioned to be "under no obligation," we spend most of our lives running from responsibility and resisting any and all efforts to hold us accountable.

1. We build loopholes into our laws and put escape clauses into our contracts.
2. We get out of bad debts by filing for bankruptcy and out of bad marriages by filing for divorce.
3. The prospect of having to answer to God is a thought from which we steadfastly recoil.

B. But, whether we like it or not, the God of the Bible is a God who judges His creatures.
   1. The God of creation is also the God of the flood.
   2. The shepherd who lays down his life for His sheep is also the shepherd who will separate the sheep from the goats.

C. According to our text, God's scrutiny of us penetrates to the inner man to examine "the thoughts and attitudes of the heart." There are at least two reasons why God focuses on our hearts.
   1. According to the Bible, the "heart" is the seat of human intellect and will. It is that part of us that dreams and schemes, that plans and decides. It is, therefore, the source of human behavior.
   2. A man's heart does not always match his habits. It is only when we know the heart behind the habit that we know the real person.

Conclusion

As any recovering alcoholic will tell you, the first step toward recovery is the honest admission of the problem. Being exposed can be a painful experience, but it can also be a redemptive experience. It peels away the layers of pretense behind which we hide, and it enables us to present our true selves unto God.

Illustration

In C.S. Lewis' fantasy, *Chronicles of Narnia,* the character Eustace is saved from his dragonish ways by being "undressed" by a huge lion (the Christ figure in the *Chronicles*) and then plunged into water. With great fear Eustace endured the pain of the lion's claw as it tore layer after layer of dragon's skin until he recovered his real self. This portrait of redemption is close to the one presented in this text.

Father, I Have Sinned

Luke 15:17-20

Introduction

"I have sinned," cried the prodigal. For him those words did not come easily. It seems they never do. In fact as far as the biblical record is concerned, the confession "I have sinned" occurs only seven times in the English Bible. And even in these few cases it took a lot of convincing before the guilty party was willing to admit it (*e.g.* Pharoah, Aachan, Balaam, David).

It's not any easier for people to admit it today. In fact, our culture has de-theologized human behavior and written the word *sin* right out of our national vocabulary. Though passé to many moderns the concept of sin is at the heart of the biblical testimony of what is wrong with man. Our text reveals two aspects of sin which are crucial for us to understand.

I. The Reality of Sin

A.   We divise new labels for old evils.

1.   What Isaiah said to the people of his day could also be said to ours: "Woe to those who call evil good" (5:20).

2.   We, like the prodigal, know something is desperately wrong with us. It's just that we no longer call it "sin." We define our problem as ignorance, sickness, deviancy, poverty, disfunction, inhumanity, crime, and perversion. But according to the Bible these are the symptoms of a deeper problem.

B.   *Sin* needs to be resurrected as a legitimate category to describe what is wrong with humankind.

1.   Human behavior cannot be judged solely on the basis of the effect it has upon others. It must also be judged on the basis of the effect it has upon God.

2.   Some sins do hurt other people. But all sin hurts God. It violates his will and rebels against his authority. As the prodigal said, *"Father,* I have sinned against *heaven* and against *you."*

3.   "For all have sinned and fall short of the glory of God." (Romans 3:23) "There is no one righteous, not even one." (Romans 3:10). That is reality. It honestly describes what is wrong with us.

II. The Remedy for Sin

A. There is something we must do.

1. "He came to his senses" (v. 17). Someone has said that when the prodigal fretted at home wanting to be away he called what he was doing "independence." Out in the far country he called it "pleasure." When he lost his money, he called it "bad luck." But when he reached bottom in the pig sty, he finally called it what it really was, "Father, I have sinned."

2. It was in this moment of truth that this lost boy began the long trek which leads back to the Father's house. "Repentance" is what the Bible calls it—being honest to self and honest to God. He acknowledged that what he was doing was wrong and admitted he needed forgiveness that only his Father could give.

B. There is something God will do.

1. Sin is never fully remedied by that which we alone can do. We can express sorrow for our sins. We can even try to make amends for our sins. But we cannot forgive ourselves of our sins.

2. That is something only God can do. It is Him we have wronged; it is His house we have forsaken for the far country.

3. And here we come to the climax of the story and the central message of the gospel. In spite of the fact that we have sinned against Him, God still loves us and wants us to come home.

Conclusion

"But while he was still a long way off, his father saw him and was filled with compassion for him" (v. 20). Do you think it was just by accident that the father was looking down the road that evening? No. He missed that boy, for he never stopped seeing him through the eyes of a loving parent. So also does God eagerly await our return to the Father's house.

The Best Thing I Know
Hebrews 1:1-3

Introduction

Dr. Howard Lowry once said that when one speaks on a significant occasion he should say the best thing that he knows. That is why I would speak to you of Jesus. This is exactly what the author of Hebrews was doing all through his epistle.

I. The early church needed to be reminded of its best thing.

The Hebrew Christians, after years of unrelenting persecution, were beginning to focus on some of the church's good things at the expense of its best thing.

A. Some were wanting to follow angels. Angels do God's bidding, deliver His messages and watch over His children. Angels are good things, admits the author, but they are not the best thing. Follow Jesus.

B. Some were wanting to cling to their religious heritage and focus on the founders of their faith—Moses, Joshua and Aaron. But, as the author reminds them, the word of Christ is greater than any law of Moses, His promised land is greater than the one to which Joshua led Israel, and His priesthood is superior to Aaron's. These are good men, but they are not the best man. Follow Jesus.

C. Some were looking to religious institutions—the temple and its rituals. But, as the author reminds them, the earthly temple is but a shadow of a greater one in heaven, and its sacrifices are just an illustration of and preparation for the far greater sacrifice of Jesus Christ. These are good things, but they are not the best thing. Follow Jesus.

D. Some were turning to theology, focusing on the fundamentals of the faith. They sought to define themselves, identify themselves with what the author calls the "elemental truths" of the faith (6:1-2). But the writer suggests that, as good as this list is, they need to be going on to other things. This list is a good thing, but it is not the best thing. Follow Jesus.

II. The modern church still needs to be reminded of its best thing.

A.   The church today still has a penchant for focusing on its good things at the expense of its best thing.

1.   We focus more on the preacher than the Living Word, the sacraments more than the Saviour, the process of worship more than the Person who is to be worshipped.

2.   Loyalty that belongs to Christ is pledged instead to his ministers. Trust that should be placed in Christ is instead placed in theological systems which seek to define Him.

B.   Perhaps it is time we took all of the good things of Christianity and laid them, humbly and submissively, at the feet of the best thing.

III. Jesus is still the church's best thing.

A.   History validates the greatness of Jesus. True greatness belongs to Him; not to the weak pretenders we make our idols.

1.   Sports legends, entertainers, politicians, popular religionists—none of them can compare with Jesus. He alone is without peer.

2.   But Jesus is more than the greatest man. He is the very Son of God. He is in every way the incomparable Christ.

B.   Only Jesus can save us.

1.   Mere mortals cannot save us, no matter how powerful, influential, noble or kind. Churches cannot save us, no matter how correct their doctrine or fervent their zeal.

2.   Even the cross alone cannot save us, no matter how brutal and unjust the act wrought upon it or how undeserving the victim.

3.   The cross saves because of who was on it—"God was in Christ reconciling the world unto Himself."

Conclusion

There are many good things about the church. But if you are looking for the greatest thing, the most glorious thing, the best thing, then I would point you to Jesus. Jesus is the best thing I know.

Journey's End

John 14:1-6

Introduction

In the long ago the biblical psalmist cried, "Show me, O Lord, my life's end" (Psalm 39:4). That is a good prayer for our times. For a person to make life's journey meaningful and worthwhile he must have at least two things in sight: a destination, somewhere to go; and a direction, a way to get there. Jesus speaks of both in our text.

I. The Destination — "to the Father."

A. Any journey that is worthwhile must have a destination.

1. To depart without a destination is to doom oneself to aimless wandering.

2. One of the great tragedies of our times is that we do not know where we are going. When we move into the future, we leave no forwarding address.

3. We would do well to heed the words of Moses to a people wandering aimlessly in the wilderness, "If only they were wise and would . . . discern what their end will be!" (Deuteronomy 32:29)

B. A journey that is worthwhile must have the right destination.

1. "There is a way that seems right to man, but in the end it leads to death" (Proverbs 14:12).

2. Not all goals we pursue in life are the right ones. Many of the things we seek most really are not worth the effort.

3. Such, Jesus said, is the case with the man who lays up treasures on earth (Luke 12:13-21).

4. According to Jesus there is only one destination that is truly worthwhile—the Father's house.

II. The Direction - "no one comes to the Father except through me."

A. Some people who have the Father's house in their sights never get there because they get lost on some side street.

1. Some people try to get there by living the "good, moral life."

2. Some people try to get there by following their own "gospel."

3. Some people try to get there by being "religious."

B. But, according to Jesus, there is only one way to the Father's house.
   1. In our pluralistic society we do not like exclusiveness. We like inclusiveness. We like to treat every religion as good, every philosophy as worthwhile.
   2. For us the ultimate virtue is toleration. We are quick to brand those who preach the "one way" as bigoted and intolerant.
   3. Yet we have these words of Jesus, "No one comes to the Father except through me."

C. The exclusiveness of Christianity comes from its founder.
   1. It is not *our* intolerance, it is *His*. It is not *our* narrowness, it is *His*.
   2. Just as we have no right to make the way narrower than He does, we have no right to make it broader than he does.

D. It is the exclusiveness of Christianity that makes evangelism an imperative of the church.
   1. It is why Christ commissioned His followers to preach the gospel to every creature.
   2. It is why Paul was driven to take the gospel to his world.
   3. It is why the church still confronts an often indifferent world and boldly preaches that Jesus saves.

Conclusion
If you get where you are going, where will you be?

Illustrations:
Read Robert Frost's, "The Road Not Taken."

Socrates once walked the streets of Athens and accused his countrymen of living the "unexamined life." He might well have walked the streets of America.

Present-tense Christianity

Hebrews 3:7-4:11

Introduction

Christianity is not a noun. It is a verb. It is about what God *has done, is doing,* and *will do.* It is about what we *were, are,* and *shall be.* It is more than an institution; it is an action, a state of being.

In our text the author explores the three tenses of Christianity. Three times he quotes from Psalm 95:7—"Today, if you hear his voice, do not harden your hearts"— in an effort to motivate his readers to live for today in light of the lessons of the past and the promises of the future.

I. Learn from the Past (3:8).

A. These Christians, like all of us, came to Christ out of a "past."

    1. A past is a hard thing to shake. It is something you are always trying to live up to or to live down.

    2. Some of us are proud of our pasts, but most of us are prisoners to them.

B. The only proper way to deal with the past is to learn from it.

    1. You can try to live in the past or you can try to run from the past; but you can never truly forget the past.

    2. Since we cannot leave the past behind, perhaps at least we can learn from it. This is exactly what the author tells us to do. "You are your fathers' sons," he says, "but you do not need to repeat your fathers' sins."

II. Long for the Promised (4:9).

A. There is a sense in which Christianity is a religion of the "by-and-by."

    1. Nothing is more basic to biblical Christianity than what it hopes for hereafter.

    2. The second-coming, heaven, hell, punishment, reward—all are major tenets of a faith that proclaim, "This world is not my home."

B. Christians live their lives expectantly, awaiting the fulfillment of God's promises.

    1. "Hope" and "trust" are future-tense verbs. By them we

anticipate the promises of God.

2. For the Christian the past is forgiven and the present empowered by what is to come.

3. According to our author our labor for the Lord will be consummated by a "Sabbath rest." The career of faith has an end of finished work, fulfilled hope, and realized destiny.

III. Live in the Present (3:14).

A. Ours is a religion of the present tense, a "here-and-now" religion of what is.

1. It is about conviction and conduct, believing and behaving in response to God's call.

2. Christianity is a process. There is a sense in which we are ever "becoming" Christian.

B. God is concerned about more than what we have done for Him. He is concerned about what we have done for Him *lately*.

1. "Today," insists our author, "today, if you will hear his voice do not harden your hearts."

2. Refusing to let us "rest on our laurels," God continually confronts us with some moment of truth to which we must respond. In our response we demonstrate our faithfulness to Him.

Conclusion

"Believe" and "obey" are present-tense verbs. They are what we do between Egypt and Canaan, between redemption and final rest. "Today, if you will hear his voice, harden not your hearts."

Illustrations

"History repeats itself." It has to. Nobody listens.

A wise preacher once responded to a bitter woman's resentful cry with words that capture the essence of Christianity as a "present-tense" religion. Angry at God over what had happened to her, she defiantly protested, "I wish I had never been made." To which the preacher replied, "You have not been made, you are still being made."

Lord, Teach us to Pray

Luke 11:1-12; 22:39-42

Introduction

A surprising number of Christians never do develop a healthy prayer life. Prayer is often reduced to little more than a polite formality before meals, or a hasty word at the end of the day, or a last resort, when they have nowhere else to turn.

This is quite a contrast to Christ. His was a life of prayer. His disciples took note of it and asked Him to teach them to pray.

In Jesus' response to their request we can learn at least two things about prayer.

I. Prayer Requires Effort.

A. According to Jesus, it is when prayer is persistent that it is effective.

1. In this humorous story of a man pounding on his neighbor's door at midnight, Jesus presents prayer as a profound, persistent exercise (vv. 5-8).

2. Some Christians might seek to use prayer as a substitute for Christian duty and responsibility.

B. True prayer can be an agonizing work experience.

1. It is something that pulls out of one's soul the great resources we have and attaches them to the even greater resources of God.

2. Meaningful prayer expects things of the one praying as well as anticipating things from God.

II. Prayer Requires Faith.

A. Effective prayer requires faith that there is Someone listening.

1. I'm convinced that some people, even some Christians, do not pray because they really do not believe anyone is listening.

2. They see God as distant, aloof, and unconcerned with what is going on in the insignificant little lives of individual people.

3. The Bible, however presents a different picture of God. He is portrayed as responsive and most interested in what His

children have to say. In comparing the Heavenly Father to their earthly fathers, Jesus asks his disciples, "If you know how to give good gifts to your children, how much more will your Father in heaven give the Holy Spirit to those who ask him?"

B. Effective prayer requires the kind of faith that can accept God's answer.
   1. The Bible makes great claims for the power of prayer.
      a. Abraham prayed and God healed Abimelech.
      b. Hannah prayed and she received a child.
      c. Elijah prayed and it did not rain.
      d. Hezekiah prayed and his life was extended fifteen years
      e. The disciples prayed and Peter was released from prison.
      f. James 5:16; I Peter 3:12
   2. Yet some of us are not so sure of this. We have prayed for things and not received them, leaving some of us to wonder if God really answers prayer.
   3. But just because we do not always get what we want in prayer does not mean that our prayers go unanswered. There are other answers besides "yes."
   4. God said "no" to the prayer of Paul that his "thorn in the flesh" might be removed. He also said "no" to the prayer of his Son that He be allowed to escape the cross. Yet God was able turn those "no's" into even greater, unexpected blessings.
   5. The real challenge of prayer is not to demand things of God, but to submit ourselves unto God; not to try to use Him, but to be used of Him.

Conclusion

There is no limit to what God can do to an individual Christian or to a church who will exercise this form of disciplined, believing, persistent prayer. Jesus said, "My house shall be called a house of prayer." When it is, it will be a house of power.

Illustration

Dwight L. Moody once said, "Every great movement of God can be traced to a kneeling figure."

Going the Second Mile
Matthew 5:38-48

Introduction

"If someone forces you to go one mile . . . ." This expression came out of old Persia and refers to the authority given by the king to those sent to do his bidding. If a courier or soldier needed assistance in fulfilling the king's mission, he could commandeer any man or horse or wagon with no questions asked. Later the armies of the Greeks and the Romans adopted the practice.

In Jesus' day any Jew could be forced away from his own concerns to help a legionnaire who may or may not have really needed him. In much the same way Simon of Cyrene was "compelled," (forced) to bear the cross of Jesus (Matthew 27:32).

The Jews of Jesus' day, of course, deeply resented this humiliating law and saw it as a symbol of foreign domination. You can imagine, then, their surprise when Jesus said, "go with him two miles."

I. A One-mile World

"If someone forces you . . . strikes you . . . sues you . . . asks you" (Matthew 5:38-42).

A. This saying is hard on us because we, like the Jews of the first century, live in a one-mile world.
   1. It is a world of rights and responsibilities.
   2. It is a world of basic criteria and minimum standards.

B. Our concept of "justice" is built on the principle of "reciprocity." It seeks to insure that those who violate rights and deny justice are appropriately punished.
   1. "An eye for an eye," is the way the Bible puts it. Rather than inviting retaliation, the real goal of this law was to insure justice by guaranteeing proportional compensation to the victim. It was designed to keep the rich and powerful from literally "getting away with murder."
   2. Such justice is sanctioned by God Himself as a means of constraining the human tendency toward exploitation and manipulation of the defenseless.

C. Understanding this, we are even more surprised at these words of Jesus.

1. Rather than calling upon them (and us) to resist this unjust law or, at best, to comply with it only minimally, he calls upon his followers to respond to evil with good and to domination with voluntary subordination.
2. To citizens of a one-mile world this just does not compute.

II. A Second-mile Church

"Turn the other cheek . . . give your last garment . . . go the extra mile . . . love your enemies" (Matthew 5:38-48)

A. At this point I am desperate to explain how this text does not mean what it really says.
    1. I would like to appeal to "oriental exaggeration" or "rhetorical hyperbole" as a way to diffuse the power of these words to my life. I would like to do this but I can't.
    2. Though Jesus does not expect a slavishly literal application of the examples He offers (see John 18:22,23; Matthew 21:12-17), it is none-the-less clear that He is calling for a new and different response to the people who try to exploit us.

B. What does it mean to "go the second mile?"
    1. It means to rise above the instinctive desire to "strike back," "get even," or "settle the score" and to meet evil with good.
    2. It means to swallow pride and abandon self-interest. It means to be slow to anger and quick to forgive. It means to live by grace in the face of the unfair.

C. Why should we do this?
    1. To master the power of passive resistance? To shame the sinner into repentance? To these potential benefits Jesus does not appeal.
    2. Do this, He says, because God acts like this toward us (see Matthew 5:45; also Romans 5:7).

Conclusion

Before we dismiss the ethic of the second mile as "ideal" or "unworkable" we should remember how close it is to the gospel.

He Must Become Greater, I Must Become Less

John 3:22-31

Introduction

While John was at the peak of his career, Jesus appeared on the scene and the crowds, who had once streamed out of the villages to follow John, began to follow Jesus instead. As John watched them go, his only response was, "He must become greater, I must become less."

John's response to Christ is the same response which all of us must offer Him. John was able to do this because:

I. He Mastered Himself — "I must become less."

A. The desire for recognition is a universal human drive.
   1. We all want to be important, to surpass others, to achieve distinction.
   2. This desire often drives much that we do in life.

B. Unchecked or improperly channeled this instinct can get us into a lot of trouble.
   1. Even good deeds can be undone by an overeager desire for credit and self-acclaim.
   2. At its worst it can even become ruthless. History is strewn with the wreckage of the havoc visited upon us by people who have reached for greatness with no respect for God or fellow humans.

C. Even the church suffers from unchecked or improperly channeled egos.
   1. Ego-centric preachers, ruling elders, resident critics—all trying to impose their will upon the kingdom of God.
   2. The unbridled ego may be the single greatest threat to the health of the church.

D. Properly channeled, however, this powerful human instinct can be the source of great achievement.
   1. In response to the egotistical request of James and John to sit at His right hand (Mark 10-35-45), Jesus urged them to seek true greatness through service
   2. Christian greatness is a greatness that undergirds rather than overpowers, that seeks to serve rather than to be served.

3. This is the greatness John the Baptizer rose to in this, his most difficult moment.

II. He Was Mastered By Jesus Christ — "He must become greater."

A. When John looked at Jesus, he saw something in Him which he himself did not possess, something with which he could not compare.
   1. He noticed it in his preaching.
   2. He witnessed it in his miracles.
   3. But it went even deeper. He saw it in his person.

B. True greatness belongs only to Jesus.
   1. History validates his greatness. He alone is without peer.
   2. Jesus was more than the greatest man. He is the Son of God. According to the scriptures it is He who: made the world, sustains the world, saves the world, presides over the world. He is in every way the incomparable Christ.

C. And John may have been the first person to truly sense it.
   1. When he sees Him coming to the Jordan, there is no question in his voice: "Behold the Lamb of God who takes away the sin of the world!"
   2. With these words John acknowledges Jesus as more than the master teacher, more than the great physician, more than a great humanitarian. He is uniquely the Savior of the world.

Conclusion

For John, to meet Jesus was to be mastered by Him. So must it be for all who will answer His call to salvation and service.

Illustrations

Carl Sandburg once said, "We all want to play Hamlet."

Alfred Adler, one of the fathers of modern psychiatry, considers the desire for recognition one of the strongest of all human instincts.

Spiritual Never-never Land

Hebrews 5:11-6:3

Introduction

Peter Pan is J. M Barrie's classic tale of a boy who refuses to become a man. In similar fashion some Christians refuse to grow up in Christ. According to our text spiritual maturation requires a progression:

I. From Learning to Living

You are slow to learn . . . being still an infant . . . not acquainted with the teaching about righteousness (Hebrews 5:11,13).

A. Some Christians suffer from a learning disability. This was the case for the Hebrew Christians.
   1. The problem was not an intellectual one; it was spiritual.
   2. Their ignorance was willful, evidencing itself in a conscious refusal to learn.
   3. This resulted in an arrested spiritual development. They were still in grade school when, by now, they "ought to be teachers."

B. Spiritual ignorance, willful or otherwise, is always treated as a serious problem in Scripture.
   1. The prophet Hosea warns that "a people without understanding will come to ruin" (Hosea 4:14).
   2. On numerous occasions Paul prefaced his teachings to the churches by declaring that he did not want them to be ignorant (Romans 1:13; 1 Corinthians 10:1).

C. True spirituality is a "subject" which cannot be learned in a classroom.
   1. It must be learned experentially by living in right relationship with God.
   2. Using the model of an athlete who systematically trains to compete, he suggests that righteousness is acquired through regular practice (5:14).

II. From Lingering to Leaving

Therefore let us leave the elementary teachings about Christ and go on to maturity (Hebrews 6:1).

A. Some Christians prefer the security of perpetual preparation for service to the challenges of actually living for Christ in a sometimes hostile world.
   1. Instead of building upon the foundations of their faith, they continue to lay those foundation again and again.
   2. Instead of seeking new experiences in Christian living, they are content to repeat the old ones.

B. A religion is a good place to hide from God.
   1. Affirming doctrine is much easier than living in devotion.
   2. Performing liturgy is much easier than practicing piety.

C. There is no "status quo" in righteousness.
   1. To stand still is to begin to slip backwards.
   2. As the author goes on to warn (6:4-12) arrested spiritual development may ultimately lead to apostasy.

Conclusion

Peter Pan is a charming plot for a play, but it is a crippling plot for a life. Those who follow this path never reach their spiritual potential. The gospel calls us to grow in Christ continually.

Illustration

As a college teacher I once enrolled a student in a class only later to learn that he had just completed a similar course at another college. When I asked him why he was willing to invest time and energy in a class he had already taken, he replied, "Because I know I can do well in it. I won't have to study in order to pass." Five years later, this same student was still taking classes even though he had enough credits to graduate. Preferring the inherent security of his educational "nest" to the unpredictable and imposing "real world," he was intentionally prolonging the preparation phase of his life at the expense of the productive phase. Some Christians do much the same in the church.

We Have This Treasure

2 Corinthians 4:7

Introduction

Some of the world's most priceless treasures have been placed in its most worthless containers. But the contrast between treasure and vessel was never greater than when God committed the saving gospel of His Son to mortal men, when His extraordinary truth was committed to such an ordinary church.

I. The Treasure

A. The gospel is the one great treasure of the church.

   1. It is the "pearl of great price" for which the jeweler will pay all that he has (Matthew 13:45-46).

   2. It is the great truth for which Stephen died and which Paul devoted his life to proclaim.

   3. It is the one thing which clearly distinguishes the church from all other religious and benevolent organizations.

B. The church today, however, does not always prize the gospel as its greatest treasure.

   1. The church is sometimes tempted to emphasize its own human dynamics rather than that which God offers us in Jesus Christ.

   2. The church sometimes calls people to its ministry, its programs, or to its facilities instead of calling people to salvation in Jesus Christ.

II. The Vessel

A. Though we would expect the world's greatest treasure to be placed in its most priceless container, we find the gospel committed to a very ordinary church.

   1. The Corinthian church to which Paul wrote was a handful of converted slaves and artisans, an unimpressive lot—hardly the cream of the social crop. These are those of whom Paul admitted, "not many wise, not many mighty, not many noble are called."

    2.   Paul, himself, was a most "earthen vessel"—haunted by his past, crippled by his inadequacies, continually challenged by his never-ending struggle with temptation.

B.   The church today is still very "earthen."
1. It is crippled by its lack of commitment, its divisions, its worldliness.
2. Its ministry is sometimes weak, susceptible to burnout and moral failure.

III. Dealing with the Disparity

A.   Some people are not content to allow the contrast to exist.
1. Some would try to accept the treasure but reject the jar. They say yes" to Christ but "no" to the church, and in the process scorn the very ones for whom Christ died.
2. Others try to make the treasure more like the vessel, stripping Christ of His divinity.
3. Still others try to make the vessel more "worthy" of the treasure by changing the clay pot into a silver chalice. This leads to a situation where the vessel takes on more importance than the treasure.

B.   The proper response is to acknowledge the disparity and learn the great lesson which it teaches.
1. The disparity is there by God's design to demonstrate that it is upon human weakness, not human strength that God chooses to build His church.
2. God can use the church best when it depends less on its own resources and learns to trust in the power of the God who alone can save.

Conclusion

Charles Haddon Spurgeon used to address candidates for the ministry as they prepared to graduate from seminary. He would always conclude his sermon by asking them an all-important question. It is the same question I would ask of you in closing today: "Do you have this treasure?"

Win the Lost at Any Cost

1 Corinthians 2:1-5

Introduction

There are many noble pursuits in life, but there is at last one which towers over all the rest, that causes all others to stand in its shadow. It is one of the very reasons for the church's existence. It is not an invitation, it is an imperative. It comes not from man but from Christ Himself. It is to this task that I would call the church.

"Go ye into all the world and preach the gospel." Win the lost at any cost.

In our text we find the testimony of a man who answered this call. His response may be seen as a model for our own.

I. The Man

For there to be evangelism, there must be an evangelist. What kind of person can God use?

A. One who is willing to go. "When I came," said Paul.
    1. The early church took the great commission seriously. They began at Jerusalem and they went. On the street corners and in the market places, whenever and wherever the message needed to be heard, they "declared it publicly and house-to-house."
    2. It seems today that somehow that divine commission has lost some of its urgency. Instead of winning the world to Christ we have become content to gather regularly and talk about winning the world.

B. One who is willing to be used in spite of his fears and shortcomings.
    1. Paul confesses that he was with them in "weakness" and "fear." He understood the natural fear we have of confronting someone with a message that we are not even sure that he wants to hear.
    2. Paul was also keenly aware of his personal limitations, his lack of "eloquence" and "wisdom." This illustrates that the real ability that God blesses is "usability."

II. The Manner

A. Evangelism is to be done with integrity not with clever manipulation, not with "wise and persuasive words."

    1. Many people are turned off by the mere mention of "evangelism" because of the bad name some non-scrupulous, pseudo-religionists have given it. In some cases today it has been reduced to cheap promotionalism.

    2. That is not how Paul came to the Corinthians (see also 2 Corinthians 4:2) His witness was genuine and sincere.

B. Evangelism is to be done with primary dependency upon God rather than man. It is to be done "in demonstration of the Spirit's power." It is, after all, God who "gives the increase."

III. The Message — "Jesus Christ and him crucified"

A. There was once a great conviction that gripped the church of Jesus Christ—that Jesus Christ is the only savior of humankind and that apart from Him people are lost and doomed to destruction.

    1. So important was this to Paul that he said, "Woe is me if I preach not the gospel."

    2. So important was it to Henry Martyn that when he landed on the shores of India he said, "Here let me burn myself out for God."

B. In our sophisticated society we seldom find salvation worth talking about any more.

    1. The church is involved in too many other things that come at the expense of the proclamation of the gospel.

    2. Ours is not the age of the rejection of the gospel. It is the age of the unproclaimed gospel.

Conclusion

How many of us in the room today have spoken to a lost person about Jesus Christ in the last week, month, year, in the entire time we have been a Christian? If not us, then who? If not now, then when?

Illustration

H.L. Hendricks once said that he could not find a single verse of Scripture that commands a lost person to go to church but he could quote numerous scriptures that call the church to go a lost world.

The Ministry of the Encouragers

Acts 4:36-37; 9:26-30; 15:1-41

Introduction

In biblical times names did more than simply distinguish one person from another. They had meaning, they stood for something—sometimes for the very essence of the people who wore them.

Take the name "Barnabas" for example. His original name was "Joseph," but because of a certain graciousness about him the apostles gave him the nickname of "Barnabas." It means "son of encouragement." What a great name! Barnabas was known for his willingness to seek out those who were struggling and encourage them along in the work of the Lord.

In what ways can the ministry of the encouragers bless the church today?

I. Getting People into the Church

A. Barnabas helped Paul find acceptance by the church in Jerusalem (Acts 9:26-30).

    1. The newly converted Saul of Tarsus was, at first, denied fellowship by the church in Jerusalem.

    2. But Barnabas believed in his conversion story and helped him find a home with the believers.

    3. All that Paul was later to do and write might have been lost had Barnabas not been there to help him find a home in the church.

B. Barnabas helped the Gentiles find equal acceptance with the Jews in the first century church (Acts 15:1-35).

    1. Some Jews were refusing to admit the Gentiles as equal members. They were insisting that they become Jews before they could become Christians.

    2. Barnabas, along with Paul, stood up for the Gentile believers and helped them have equal access to the gospel and its blessings.

C. The church still needs sons and daughters of encouragement to stand at her open doors today.

    1. How many "Pauls" never make it into the church because of its fear of outsiders?

2. How many people of other races and classes never make it into the church because of its slowness to accept those who are "different"?

II. Keeping People in the Church

A. Barnabas encouraged John Mark in a way that may have saved him for meaningful service (Acts 9:36-40).
1. John Mark had failed Paul and Barnabas on their first missionary journey, and Paul was not willing to give him another chance.
2. But Barnabas believed in Mark and took him along with him on his own separate journey in order to encourage Mark in the Lord's service.
3. All that John Mark was later to do for the Lord might have been lost had Barnabas not been there for him in that difficult time.

B. Such encouragement can keep people in the church today.
1. People are still failing and growing discouraged in their efforts to live for Christ. Some of them even leave the fellowship of the church.
2. Such people can be saved and restored to meaningful service through the ministry of encouragement.

Conclusion

The church needs the ministry of evangelists, of elders, of deacons, of teachers and a host of other functions. But perhaps what it needs most is the ministry of the encouragers—people who will be quick to catch the faltering and call home the lost.

Illustrations

"What's in a name?" asked William Shakespeare. Sometimes a lot more than meets the eye. These lines from the hymn "Rescue the Perishing" express the potential good that can come from encouragement.

"Down in the human heart, crushed by the tempter, feelings lie buried that grace can restore. Touched by a loving hand, wakened by kindness, chords that were broken will vibrate once more."

Unintentional Ministry
Acts 16:25

Introduction

Most of the things we do for God we do on purpose. They are intentional, they are consciously planned. But sometimes our most meaningful ministries are performed spontaneously or unconsciously. They are not planned, they just flow out of who we are and what our lives are about.

I. The Unintentional Ministry of Paul and Silas

A. Paul and Silas came to Philippi to perform one kind of ministry, but they ended up performing another.

    1. They had come to Philippi to preach the gospel but they ended up in jail. They had come to do good but received only evil in return. They had come to set people free only to have their freedom taken away. In similar fashion, our service for God today does not always result in positive response or personal reward.

    2. But with their imprisonment came a new, unexpected, unplanned opportunity to minister. In similar fashion our planned ministries can open unexpected doors to unplanned ones. We may set out to do one thing, but God may have something else in mind.

B. Paul and Silas' response to their undeserved confinement was to worship.

    1. Instead of cursing God or crying to him as many a prisoner must have done, they chose to sing to Him songs of praise.

    2. We, too, have choices with regard to how we will respond to life's "unfair" blows. We can be broken by them or seethe in resentment over them, or we can look within them for some new reason to praise God.

C. In their worshipful response to their imprisonment they ended up performing an unintentional ministry.

    1. Paul and Silas sang because of their faith, because Christ was with them and giving them strength. They sang because they could not help but sing.

    2. And all the time, though they never dreamed it, they were

serving others better than they knew. Those around them witnessed their faith and were blessed by it.

II. Our Unconscious Ministries

A.   To be sure, the church still needs our conscious ministries. It needs our planned giving, our planned service, our carefully planned teaching and preaching and singing.

    1.   A ministry that is unplanned is often unfruitful.

    2.   Lack of conscious preparation often results in wasted and misspent resources.

B.   But some of our finest and best ministries are unconscious ministries.

    1.   That which flows from us naturally because of who we are and what we are about is sometimes our purest service.

    2.   People are sometimes more blessed by overhearing us than by hearing us. God is able to take our songs at midnight and use them to bless others.

    3.   Like Faithful of *Pilgrim's Progress* in the valley of the shadow we lift up our voices because our hearts are strong, and some poor struggling soul stumbling on behind us thanks God and takes courage to keep going toward the celestial city.

Conclusion

Our finest sermons may be the ones we live, our finest songs the ones we sing at midnight.

Illustration

When Sir Walter Scott was building his estate, he built a little summer house near the stables. He built there not because of the view but because of what it allowed him to overhear. Each evening his coachman, old Peter—a Scotsman who never publicly talked religion—would, in the privacy of his room, raise a Psalm to God. His voice was awful, and he never sang on key, but to Sir Walter it was the sweetest of sounds and by it his heart was comforted.

No young child starts his day by saying, "I'm going to be a blessing today." He is a blessing and he never even knows it. So, too, that which we do naturally and unintentionally can be a source of blessing to others.

The Social Gospel

Matthew 25:35-46

Introduction

Some have branded the "social gospel" the worst possible perversion of the church's calling, suggesting that the church should be interested only in saving people's souls, not in ministering to their earthly needs. Yet both the life and teachings of Jesus confirm that this is not the case.

I. Jesus ministered to people's physical and spiritual needs.

A. Jesus was keenly interested in the eternal, spiritual needs of people.

1. He forgave people's sins.
2. He taught spiritual truths.
3. He condemned evil.
4. He called people to godly living.
5. He died on the cross to save us.

B. But Jesus also ministered to the temporal, physical needs of people.

1. He fed the hungry.
2. He healed the sick.
3. He encouraged the struggling.
4. He raised the dead.

II. The church is called to minister to people's physical and spiritual needs.

A. The church is called to seek the eternal salvation of all people.

1. It is the Great Commission of Christ to His church.
2. It is the primary ministry of the church on earth.

B. The church is also called to minister to the earthly needs of people.

1. Christ commanded it.
2. The apostles commanded it.
3. The early church practiced it.

III. The church will be judged according to its response to human need.

A. When we think of Christ's criterion for judgment, we are most accustomed to thinking in religious categories.
    1. Correct doctrine—believing the right things, teaching the true gospel.
    2. Faithfulness to the church—attending regularly, supporting its ministry.
    3. Resisting evil—keeping the "thou shalt not's."

B. But in our text Jesus offers a different criterion.
    1. He says that the test of who is fit for the kingdom is the kind of response we make to the needy people of this world.
    2. He says that when we look upon the naked, the hungry, the sick, we should look upon them as we would look upon Him and respond accordingly.

Conclusion

If you were judged by this criterion, where would you spend eternity?

Illustration

Shalom Aleichem tells the story of an old man who was afraid of getting involved in other people's lives. The man was standing on a bus when a young man next to him asked for the time. The old man just turned away and refused to reply. After the young man moved on, the old man's friend asked him why he refused such a simple request. The old man answered, "If I had given him the time of day, next he would want to know where I was going. Then we might talk about our interests. If we did that, he might invite himself to my house for dinner. If he did he would meet my lovely daughter. If he met her, they would both fall in love. I don't want my daughter marrying someone who can't afford a watch!"

As absurd as that reasoning is, some Christians are capable of employing such logic when they seek to keep themselves free of "over-involvement" in the lives of others.

From Doubt to Faith

John 20:24-29

Introduction

Why is it that some people believe the gospel and others do not? Perhaps the experience of Thomas can supply at least some of the answers to this question. (Retell the story leading up to Thomas' encounter with the risen Christ.)

From this text we can observe three barriers to faith that Thomas had to overcome in order to believe in the resurrected Lord.

I. Ignorance

A. One of the reasons Thomas was slow to believe in the resurrection of Christ is that he did not have all the evidence.

    1. The resurrected Christ had appeared to the disciples and gladdened their hearts with his presence (John 20:19-23).

    2. But, as our text reminds us (v. 24), Thomas had not been among them. He had spent a whole week in doubt and despair because he was absent from the place where he was most likely to meet Christ. He did not expose himself to all of the evidence.

B. Thomas is the patron saint of a whole generation of doubters who have systematically detached themselves from the believing community.

    1. There are many people who seek to be good without God, a Christian without the church. Such people are ripe for doubt.

    2. The honest searcher will seek faith where other people have found it. He will expose himself to the evidence of God's reality—to the contagion of other people's faith, to the preaching and teaching of the word of God.

    3. Why is it that people who doubt God the most are often the very ones who know the least about Him?

II. Cynicism

A. Thomas was from Missouri. "Show me," was the motto of his life. Doubt was woven deep into the fabric of his life. He seems to have been cynical by nature.

      1.   In the two other glimpses John gives us of Thomas he is consistently in the role of the skeptic, fearing the worst and slow to believe (John 11:16; 14:5).

      2.   The cynicism and skepticism he displays in this third and final episode thus seem typical of his very disposition.

  B.   Like Thomas, it is harder for some people to believe today because they are cynical and skeptical in their basic approach to all of life. Sometimes the cruel and "unfair" blows of life make it difficult for people to profess any kind of faith in God. This is true of some of the more notable skeptics of recent history.

      1.   The atheism of Schopenhauer and Madelyn Murray O'Hare did not spring from a vacuum. Each suffered traumatic upbringings which, in part, shaped their response to God.

      2.   There are many people reeling from life's blows who have hardened their hearts to God and everybody else.

III. Empiricism

  A.   "Unless I see . . . touch . . . I will not believe." (v. 25) Thomas was an empiricist. He was one of those people for whom "seeing is believing."

      1.   As such he is a fitting model for our times. Since God cannot be "seen" or "heard" or "touched," some people are slow to acknowledge his existence. They have a tendency to trust only what their senses can confirm.

      2.   But so much of life is beyond that which can be perceived by our senses. We have never "smelled" an idea, "felt" a truth, put our "finger" on a thought. These realities are perceived in other ways.

      3.   Such is the nature of "spiritual" realities. Our senses can take us to the edges of life, but they cannot take us beyond this life. Faith and faith alone can take us beyond this life.

Conclusion

For us, like Thomas, the key to overcoming doubt is a personal encounter with the risen Lord. For Thomas this happened when he "saw" the Savior. For us it happens as we chose to accept the testimony of the Scriptures concerning him and trust in him to save us. "Blessed are those who have not seen and yet have believed" (v. 29).

Free to Fail

Matthew 25:24-25; Philippians 4:13

Introduction

Matthew 25:25 and Philippians 4:13 are two very different statements. One was made by a man who was afraid to fail and did nothing. The other was made by a man who was free to fail and did everything.

As far as the biblical record is concerned, some of the greatest achievements in the history of God's kingdom have come from very ordinary, imperfect people who have overcome failure to be used of God in a significant way. Their lives model some biblical principles for overcoming failure.

I. Do not try to hide or conceal your failures.

A. Some people spend their lives trying to cover-up their mistakes.
   1. They become "prisoners of pretense," retreating into fabrication and delusion.
   2. Their entire lives become a charade, a great hypocrisy.

B. The first step in overcoming our failures is to admit them.
   1. We must be willing to honestly confess them before God and seek his forgiveness and restoration (1 John 1:8-9).
   2. If there is any place where we should be able to admit our failures, it is the church. Christians are not perfect, just forgiven.

II. Do not be discouraged by your failures.

A. When you fail in life, you are in good company. Sir Walter Scott, Thomas Edison, Richard Byrd, Walt Disney all were considered failures before they went on to their greatest achievements.

B. In the Bible, too, we read of failures whom God took and used to accomplish great things in his service.
   1. He took a slave hiding as a fugitive from justice and used him to deliver an entire nation from bondage.
   2. He took a woman who failed in marriage seven times and used her to win a city to the Savior.
   3. He took a crooked tax collector and made him into an apostle and a biographer of the Christ.

4. He took a man who failed Christ in his darkest hour, denying Him three times, and used him to open the doors to the kingdom of God.

C. He can do the same thing in our lives. God does not easily give up on His children. Like the tireless potter bending over the spoiled clay, He yet desires to make something good and noble of our lives (Jeremiah 18:1ff).

III. Do not let fear of failure keep you from attempting great things for God.

A. Some people are petrified at the thought of failure.
1. They would rather face anything than the ego shattering experience of trying something and having it end in failure.
2. So they adopt a "play-it-safe" philosophy and end up not doing anything at all. Just like the steward in the story of the talents they bury their potential in the ground and end up standing before their Master with little in their hands.

B. It is not until we are free to fail that we are free to succeed.
1. No one was more free to fail than Jesus. It is impossible to look like a success when you are hanging on a cross. Yet he let it happen. In selfless abandonment to the will of God. He was free to fail in the eyes of man that He might succeed in the eyes of God.
2. If the church cannot risk failure in the sight of men, how can we succeed in the sight of God?

Conclusion

In Christ we are called to be secure enough in God's grace to conquer our fear of failure. We are called to be free enough in our faith to take the risks that bring reward.

Illustration

Abraham Lincoln suffered a string of failures before he was elected to the presidency. His country store went out of business. As a young lawyer he had trouble getting clients. He was defeated in his campaigns for the state legislature, the House of Representatives, the Senate and the Vice Presidency. Yet very few, if any, Americans have had more impact on our history than he.

On the Brink

Exodus 14:13-15

Introduction

Life (or is it God?) has a relentless way of pushing us to the brink. Through a persistent parade of obstacles and opportunities we are continually confronted with moments that demand a decision.

In our text we find that the nation of Israel stands at just such a place. Before them lie the blessings of God. Behind them gather the dust clouds of Pharaoh's chariots. God's message to a people on the brink is to:

I. Fear Not.

A. The sources of fear are two.

1. The fear of the past, in Israel's case, was the chariots of Egypt bent on revenge. In our case it is often the failures of our pasts which come back to haunt us.

2. In Israel's case, fear of the future, was the uncertainty of the wilderness. In our case it is also not knowing what the future holds.

B. The shackles of fear are obvious. Fear can discourage, even paralyze. Christians today like Israel of old sometimes find themselves trembling on the shore of some uncrossable sea.

C. The strength which dispels fear comes not from within us but from above us. It is the reassurance of the Lord of the universe: "Fear not." Only He can truly dispel fear. If God is for us, who can be against us?

II. Stand Firm.

A. The brink is a precarious place to stand. It is a place from which we, like Israel, like to run.

1. We can try to run backwards, to retreat into the security of the past. Israel entertained this idea numerous times in the wilderness.

2. We can try to run away, to escape the challenges of following God. Shallow belief and cheap religion always vanish in the face of challenge.

B.   But God's message to a people on the brink is to "stand firm."
1.   Our world is full of fleeing people. They are running from bad relationships, difficult jobs, challenging situations.
2.   But somehow, even in the face of the greatest challenge, faith takes a stand. Know who you are, trust in the God you serve and resolve that you will not be moved.

III. See the Salvation of the Lord.

A.   Though the brink is a fearful and uneasy place to stand, it is also the best place to observe what God can do.
1.   God had brought Israel to this place for the very purpose of demonstrating His power to save.
2.   The sea they saw as the edge of disaster, now becomes the threshold of salvation.

B.   God acts in decisive ways to demonstrate that it is He alone who can truly save. This is the great message of this text.
1.   For Israel, the miraculous crossing, the manna, quail, water, the defeat of the Amelekites all demonstrated this great truth.
2.   In man's extremity is God's opportunity. It is precisely when we are at our "end," when the situation seems most hopeless that God does His greatest works.

Conclusion

As we stand "on the brink" of life-changing decision, let us, like Israel of old, hear the word of God: "Fear not, stand firm, see the salvation of the Lord." It is the call of Scripture today that this people go forward by faith.

Illustration

During the difficult days of the Great Depression, half of all Americans were out of work. There were bread lines, even riots in the streets of Washington. But in the face of it a new voice was heard on the public stage. It was the voice of Franklin Roosevelt as he spoke in his first inaugural address in 1933. He stood on braces, a cripple leading a crippled nation. But he spoke with reassurance and gave the fearful nation a new hope when he said, "The only thing we have to fear is fear itself." The word of a president dispelled the panic of America.

In an even greater way the word of God dispels the fears of believers.

Winning Over Worry
Matthew 6:25-34

Introduction

Today America is in the grips of an epidemic of worry. We worry about money, relationships, appearance, health, what other people think of us. The symptoms of our anxiety are staggering—from emotional disorders to serious health problems. We are literally worrying ourselves to death.

There is much that we in the church have to learn about anxiety. Our worries have a way of following us into the sanctuary and sitting with us in the pew.

In our text Jesus identifies four sources of worry and suggests some strategies for coping with worry in our daily lives.

I. We worry about things over which we have no control (v.27).

    A.   There are some things which are simply beyond our control.

        1.   We could not do anything about them even if we tried.

        2.   Worrying about them not only does not change them; it also robs us of our ability to deal with then when they come.

    B.   Jesus' solution to this source of worry is implied in verse 26.

        1.   Simply stated, we must learn to accept them. We must learn to master the art of Christian resignation; learn to be content in all things.

        2.   We should pray for the courage to change what we can; the patience to accept what we cannot change; and the wisdom to know the difference.

II. We worry about things that do not really matter (v.25b).

    A.   Jesus points out that some things are more important than others.

        1.   Many of the things we worry about are simply not worth the effort.

        2.   "Much ado about nothing," is the way Shakespeare put it.

    B.   Jesus says we can conquer worry over the unimportant by learning to "seek first the kingdom of God."

        1.   The Greek word for *worry* literally means to "be pulled in different directions."

2. By aiming our lives in one direction and learning to put first things first we can reduce some of the artificial, self-made anxieties of life.

III. We worry tbout things that have not yet happened (v.34).
A. "What if" are the two most worry-filled words in the English language.
1. Anxious speculation over the future does not empty tomorrow of its trials, but it does empty today of its joys.
2. Even when we *know* something is going to happen, our fear and dread of it is almost always worse than the thing itself.

B. Christ's answer to worry over the future is found in verse 34, "Each day has enough trouble of its own." In other words, live one day at a time. Prudently manage today and let tomorrow take care of itself.

IV. We worry about things of legitimate concern.
A. As this text suggests there are some challenges of life that are of real substance.
1. There are the physical necessities of food, clothing, shelter.
2. There are the difficult circumstances that can threaten us.

B. Yet Jesus says even these things are not worthy of worry because they are things God is perfectly willing and able to assist us with.
1. "Your heavenly Father knows your needs."
2. He promises that if we seek first His kingdom, these genuine needs will be supplied.

Conclusion
"Do not be anxious about anything, but in everything by prayer and petition, with thanksgiving, present your request to God. And the peace of God which transcends all explanation will guard your hearts and minds in Christ Jesus" (Philippians 4:6, 7).

Illustration
It is said of Alexander the Great that of all the things that might have worried him, the one thing that bothered him most was that he could not get ivy to grow in Babylon. It seems we have not learned much since Alexander.

Dealing with Discouragement
1 Kings 19

Introduction

Tell the story of Elijah's flight from Jezebel and the circumstances which led up to the events of 1 Kings 19.

In our text God comes to minister to the despairing prophet. His counsel can also help us in our moments of deep discouragement.

I. God tells Elijah to attend to his own physical well-being (vv 5-8).

A. Low spirits are often the results of low physical vitality.

    1. This was the case for Elijah. He was exhausted from his recent struggles with Ahab, Jezebel, and the prophets of Baal.

    2. We, too, can succumb to moods of despondency when we are depleted of our energy—physically and emotionally exhausted.

B. God ministers to his basic physical needs for rest and rejuvenation in preparation for ministering to his deeper emotional and spiritual needs.

    1. The Bible is interested in the whole person. While the spiritual side of man is emphasized, the physical side of him is not ignored.

    2. Likewise, the church should not be drawn into an incorrect and unnecessary choice between ministering only to the spirit and not to the body. Jesus ministered to both.

II. God helped Elijah change his way of thinking (9-14,18).

A. God helped Elijah shift his thinking from self to others.

    1. Despair is essentially selfish. It is preoccupation with *my* problem, *my* difficulty. Notice the emphasis on "I, me, my" in Elijah's words.

    2. God helps Elijah contextualize his own struggles within the framework of others in his same predicament (v. 18).

    3. Seeing our own troubles in the context of suffering humanity can help us avoid some of the self-pity associated with despair.

B. God helped Elijah shift his thinking from himself to God.

 1. All of his life Elijah had associated God's reality and presence with the miraculous—sustenance by ravens, raising the widow's son, fire from heaven, etc.

 2. The purpose of the theophany at Horeb was to show Elijah that God is present in all of life. It was designed to teach him that the same presence which had been manifested in the spectacular (wind, earthquake, like the earlier fire from heaven) could also be manifested in unspectacular ways (the gentle whisper).

 3. We too need to look for God in the ordinary as well as in the spectacular and the miraculous.

III. God assigned Elijah a manageable task (vv 15-17).

God ordered Elijah to anoint the next kings of Israel (Jehu) and Syria (Hazael) and the next prophet (Elisha) through whom God would continue to act. This assignment ministered to Elijah in two important ways.

A. It helped him move from the unmanageable to the manageable.

 1. Elijah's despair was fed by a "Messiah" complex. He felt that he and he alone could solve Israel's problems (vv 10,14).

 2. By assigning him these ordinary tasks God brings him back into the world of what he can really do.

 3. Our own despair can be dispelled by returning to the world of the manageable.

B. It helped him see that he is but part of a much larger divine agenda that transcends any one personality—king or *prophet*.

 1. Elijah is gently helped to see that the will of God will continue to unfold whether or not Ahab, Jezebel, or even Elijah is still on the scene.

 2. He is but a small part of a much greater enterprise. As such, his role, which both preoccupies him and frustrates him, shrinks in its significance.

 3. We, too, need to see our problems in the context of the unfolding will of God.

Conclusion

God is there for us like he was for Elijah in life's difficult struggles as well as its spectacular victories.

Living with Loneliness

John 16:32

Introduction

We all know what it is like to feel lonely. Loneliness is Friday night with nowhere to go, eating lunch by yourself, saying "no" when everyone else is saying "yes," having no one to talk to, having the sole responsibility for making an important decision, losing a loved one.

The Bible even portrays Hell as a form of loneliness, as eternal separation from God.

Jesus can help us meet and manage the threat and pain that loneliness can bring to our lives.

I. Jesus understands our loneliness — "You will leave me alone . . . ."

A. Jesus witnessed the loneliness of others. During His earthly ministry He saw it in the eyes of lepers, heard it in the voices of the blind, and felt it in the touch of the pressing masses.

B. But even further, as our texts reminds us, Jesus Himself was left alone.

   1. We do not usually think of Jesus as being alone. We see Him in crowed streets, teaching with multitudes before Him.

   2. But we also need to see Him in Gethsemane in prayer, on trial before Pilate, climbing the hill of Calvary. The loneliness of leadership, of not being understood, of being abandoned and rejected—He knew them all.

II. Jesus teaches us the true meaning of loneliness — "You will leave me alone. Yet I am not alone . . . ."

A. We commonly associate loneliness with isolation. Yet, in this text Jesus distinguishes between the two.

   1. We often surround ourselves with crowds to keep from being lonely. But, in reality, crowds can be very lonely places.

   2. By the same token, isolation does not necessarily result in loneliness.

B. For the spiritually healthy, solitude provides an occasion to cultivate our relationship with God.

1. Jesus sought the solitude of the desert and the garden to meditate upon the will of God for his life.

2. Paul received revelations in the desert of Arabia.

3. Many saints through the ages have cherished their solitary moments for the opportunities they present to reflect on spiritual things.

C. Why then is the pain of being alone so great for so many people?

1. Is it because of the emotional pain we associate with rejection?

2. Or is it because of the company it leaves us with?

III. Jesus shows us the way to live with loneliness — ". . . for the Father is with me."

A. We, like Jesus, can live with loneliness by abiding in the presence of the Father.

1. By faith, Jesus knew God was with Him even though all others might abandon Him.

2. He promises His own continued presence for those who go forth to serve Him (Matthew 28:20).

B. We can also live with loneliness by sharing in the fellowship of the believing community (Matthew 18:20).

1. The abiding presence of Christ is actualized in the corporate worship of the church. He is there in His word, at His table.

2. The abiding presence of Christ is enjoyed in our personal interaction with those in whose lives the Spirit of Christ dwells.

Conclusion

When the church is what it should be, loving as it should love, ministering as it should minister, there should never be a lonely person in it.

Illustration

Some years ago in the city of Atlanta there was a news report circulated about two lonely women. One of them had spent $35,000 on dancing lessons just so she could be close to someone. The other, though perfectly healthy, went around town in a wheelchair with hope that someone would come along and offer to push her.

Rest for the Weary

Matthew 11:28-30

Introduction

Our age has produced a new malady. It is called "chronic fatigue syndrome." There is a sense in which all of us suffer from it. If we are nothing else, we are tired.

When we come to Christ, we come to One who can give us rest.

I. A Common Problem

A. We are all tired from something. Fatigue occasionally overtakes even the strongest among us.

1. We are tired physically and mentally from the everyday struggle to make ends meet.

2. We are tired emotionally from wrestling with dysfunctional relationships, unrealized dreams, and heartbreaking loss.

3. Ironically, we are tired spiritually from trying to live up to our faith.

B. Fatigue can do strange things to us.

1. Vince Lombardi, the great football coach, once said, "Fatigue makes cowards of us all."

2. It can even affect an entire generation, like Israel in the wilderness, breaking our resolve to go on.

II. A Comforting Promise — "I will give you rest."

A. If just anyone made this promise, we might find it empty. If a politician or even a physician made this promise, we would take it with a grain of salt. There are some things other people just can't do for us.

B. But when Jesus makes a promise, we stop and listen.

1. His promises are anything but empty. He has both the integrity and power to deliver on His word.

2. We stake our eternal destinies on the reliability of his promises. We must take this one seriously as well.

III. A Challenging Prescription — "take my yoke upon you and learn of me."

A. Jesus' next words are surprising.

1. We seek rest by escaping, getting away, relieving ourselves of responsibility.

2. Instead Jesus calls us to a new task. While we are looking for a hammock, Jesus calls us to a yoke! He calls us to find rest by voluntarily placing ourselves under a new burden.

B. Jesus' words teach us the real cause of fatigue and the nature of true rest.

1. The problem with our lives is not that we must work, that we must serve some master, perform some task. The problem is really what "work" we choose to do and whom we choose to serve.

2. The kind of rest Jesus offers is not relief from the tasks necessary to sustain us or even freedom from all of life's trials. Those early disciples who took Him up on this promise still had to labor for bread and face life's difficulties.

3. The kind of rest Jesus offers is a peace of mind, a calmness of spirit that comes from knowing our lives are being lived within His will. It is the kind of rest that accompanies a life that is rescued from self-made anxieties and stresses. Even the unavoidable work of meeting basic needs is made less tiring by the reassurance that the Savior is looking after us.

Conclusion

People wear all kinds of "yokes." Some are slaves to ambition, to greed, to materialism, to lust, to alcohol, to pride and all of its evils. These are the things that truly exhaust us. By placing ourselves under the yoke of the gentle, humble Savior our lives are liberated from the exhaustion of all these things and set free to work purposefully unto true satisfaction and fulfillment.

Illustrations

Julia Ward Howe once said that she was "tired way down into the future."

The Italian poet Dante, exiled from Florence, wandered over Europe. One night he knocked at the door of a Franciscan monastery. "What do you want? asked the monk. "Rest," replied Dante.